Lucky goes to dog school

Story by Beverley Randell

Illustrated by Warren Crossett

2

Dad and Rachel
and Lucky the dog
went to the store.

"A car is coming," said Rachel.

"Woof!" said Lucky.

"Come here, Lucky," shouted Dad.

"Come here, Lucky," shouted Rachel.

"Naughty dog!" said Dad.
"Come here!"

Dog school
Obedience class
on Saturdays
10 am

"Look at this, Rachel," said Dad.
"Look – a dog school!"

Dad and Rachel and Lucky
went in.

"Woof! Woof!" said Lucky.

"Sit," said the teacher.

Sit, Lucky," said Dad. "No, Lucky. **Sit**!"

The teacher came to help.
"Sit like this,"
he said to Lucky.
"Sit. **Sit**!"

"Woof!" said Lucky.

"Sit, Lucky," said Dad.

"Sit.

Sit, you naughty dog!

Stay with me and sit **down**!"

Dad and Rachel and Lucky
went home.

"Sit, Lucky," said Rachel.
"Sit. **Sit**!
Good dog!
Dad! Look at Lucky!"

"Good dog!"
said Dad.

"Woof, woof!"
said Lucky.